To
Karen
Happy Birthday & many
more, 13 May 2017
Love & best wishes
Frank

May the mystery of life remain ever so —

The Illustrated
Book of Zen

Publisher and Creative Director: Nick Wells
Project Editors: Catherine Taylor & Laura Bulbeck

Special thanks to Victoria Menson and Gillian Whitaker

This edition first published 2015 by
FLAME TREE PUBLISHING
6 Melbray Mews,
London SW6 3NS
United Kingdom

www.flametreepublishing.com

15 17 19 18 16
1 3 5 7 9 10 8 6 4 2

© 2015 Flame Tree Publishing Ltd

ISBN 978-1-78361-401-1

Publisher's Note:
Parts of the text of this book have been previously
published in Endless Path: Zen

Images are courtesy the following sources: Bridgeman Images and the following: 12 School of Oriental &
African Studies Library, Uni. of London; 39 & 41 Osaka Museum of Fine Arts; and Christie's: 19, 30, 37, 40,
99, 142, page numbers' decoration; iStock: 45, 82, 115, 160t; and Shutterstock.com and the following: 1 &
3 & 140 & 108 & 125 & 148 & 125 & 148/149, 17 Ola Tarakanova; 4 Romolo Tavani; 5 &150 & 151, 11, 21,
153 iBird; 9, 154 f9photos; 15, 43 & 118, 51 elwynn; 23, 29& 160b, 33, 138 Knumina Studios; 25 tang; 26
& 27 Veronika Surovtseva; 34 & 35 RG2; 46 Elina Li; 48 ARZTSAMUI; 53, 55, 63, 77, 81 fizkes; 59
mimagephotography; 61 stourn saeh; 65 Gang Liu; 67 Rido; 68 Ailisa; 73 Photobac; 74 & 75 Gelpi JM; 82
& 95 Lotus Images; 83 Nadya Lukic; 84 & 94 & 119tr Tewan Banditrukkanka; 93 colors; 97 NeydtStock;
100 isarescheewin; 102 Bashutskyy; 103 zummolo; 106 Fears; 107 gracelin; 109, 135 Sofiaworld; 110
fotohunter; 113 Banana Republic images; 117 & 119t olgaru79; 119b Rtimages; 121 bloom; 123 Nataliya
Arzamasova; 124 robert cicchetti; 126 & 144 Rita Ko; 127 Soyka; 129, 132 Vitaly Raduntsev; 131 Aleksandr
Markin; 137 Ekaterina Garyuk; 141 yienkeat; 143 ariadna de raadt; 144 VLADJ55; 156 Tabuda Y; and
Wikimedia Commons and User: Bamse/public domain 147.

A CIP record for this book is available from the British Library upon request

Printed in China | Created, Developed & Produced in the United Kingdom

The Illustrated Book of Zen

James Harrison

Introduction: David Shoji Scott

FLAME TREE
PUBLISHING

Contents

Introduction _____ 6

What is Zen? _____ 12

Zen & Now: History & Development _____ 30

Meditation: The Core of Zen _____ 48

Living Zen _____ 100

Resources _____ 158

Introduction

*T*he deepest roots of Zen are in India, where Siddhartha Gautama was born, attained enlightenment, and founded the Buddhist tradition. His life story is of more than historical interest since, for Zen followers, he is the model of one who has followed the Way to its end and achieved enlightenment. The Buddha (a Sanskrit word meaning 'Awakened One') is no abstract figure of the past, but a man with whom a Zen practitioner might feel a personal relationship in his awareness of their shared struggles. Within the Zen tradition it is understood that each of us has the potential for complete awakening, and that the Buddha's path is not reserved for a special few but is definitely open to all.

This experience of awakening embodies the realization that Buddha-nature or essential nature, or 'suchness', is inherent in all people. Based on the pragmatic experience of many seekers over many centuries, Zen is above all a practical method of how to realize this awakening and, in so doing, to see through to the essential nature of the universe and all things. For this reason, Zen has been called the 'religion before religion'.

We may substitute Tao, or God, or Ground of All Being, or another appropriate name for Buddha-nature; in this respect, the Zen tradition is a universal one. Anyone may practise it, independent of creed – indeed, the idea of being a 'Zen Buddhist' may itself, like other concepts, be discarded. A Zen characteristic, and one that separates it from other paths, is that it expresses the great matters of life and death, not in theological or metaphysical terms but in the here and now of everyday conversation and forms. Thus, when asked by a monk, 'What is the meaning of Zen?' a Zen master replied, 'Have you had your breakfast?' 'Yes', said the monk. 'Then wash your bowl', said the master. Another monk was asked the question, 'We have to dress and eat every day, and how can we escape from that?' (That is to say, how do we go on living in the world, and at the same time find liberation?) The monk replied, 'We dress, we eat.' 'I do not understand', came the reply. 'If you do not understand, put on your clothes and eat your food', said the master.

Enigmatic answers that stop the intellect are a specialty of the Zen tradition. Zen masters are not interested in metaphysical concepts, but in answers unmediated by our notions and ideas. They want answers that manifest out of the experience of our own lives; those that are – in Zen parlance – 'directly pointing at Reality'.

A pragmatic outcome of having even a partial realization or experience of one's true Nature (or Buddha-nature) is that, for many, it leads to a much greater and more active acceptance of ordinary life, and paradoxically a recognition of its extraordinary quality. Everyday activities become invested with a delightful sense of wonder.

The word Zen itself is an abbreviation of Zenna or Zenno, which is the way the Japanese would read the Chinese characters for Ch'an-na, which in its turn is Chinese for Dhyana. This is a Sanskrit word that describes both the act of meditation and the state of non-dualistic consciousness (or other states of consciousness beyond that of ordinary experience) that may arise from its practice.

As one would suspect from the origins of its name, the foundation of Zen practice is **za-zen** meditation, and its specific aim is to lead the practitioner to a full realization of his or her true nature. Zen teaches that the practice of **za-zen** is the steepest but quickest route to enlightenment, or 'seeing things as they are'. More than in any other school within the Buddhist tradition, Zen stresses the prime importance of enlightenment (you could also use the word 'realization' here) and ever-deepening enlightenment. In keeping with this, Zen requires us to drop all the various concepts onto which each of us hold in order to support the illusions that we imagine are necessary to sustain us. To this end, Zen masters make great use of contradiction and paradox. Less emphasis is placed on academic understanding, intellectual analysis and ritual than in other schools, although this does not preclude their usefulness for some people.

Japanese Zen has its origins in China, where the first Zen masters taught and the first recognizably Zen monasteries were originally founded. This sect of Buddhism was introduced to China in the sixth century and over

hundreds of years the distinctive school of Buddhism called Ch'an (pronounced Zen in Japanese) evolved. Under the Tang dynasty (618–906), also known as the Golden Age of Ch'an, this school gained particular eminence among artists and intellectuals and influenced their work and thought.

In China's Sung period (960–1276), Ch'an enjoyed wider popularity as well as government favour and won a following among all classes of people, spreading to Japan, Korea and Vietnam. Ch'an became the most powerful spiritual influence in the development of Chinese culture and Ch'an monasteries became leading centres of scholarship. In the words of the influential English writer on the subject, Alan Watts, 'The result was a tremendous cross-fertilization of philosophical, scholarly, poetic, and artistic pursuits in which the Zen and Taoist feeling of 'naturalness' became the dominant note.' The ink wash paintings of the Sung dynasty were later to have a direct influence on Japanese Zen garden design.

This Ch'an-inspired sensibility, in all its spiritual, cultural and artistic forms, was exported to Japan in the eleventh and twelfth centuries by visiting Chinese monks and by Japanese monks who had earlier travelled to China to train with Ch'an masters. With its austere practice and emphasis on intuition rather than learning, Zen had a particular appeal to the Japanese samurai, warrior classes who, in the twelfth century, replaced emperors and courtiers as the country's dominant ruling elite. The Zen tradition quickly established a powerful place in the cultural and spiritual life of its new host country and, in the course of time, developed its own unique Japanese flavour. The influence of Zen later spread throughout medieval Japanese society and may still be seen today in Japanese garden design, traditional architecture, painting, food and other specifically Japanese arts.

This book is an excellent introduction for the beginner and general reader to the fascinating tradition of Zen. Please note, however, that no book can give you a genuine taste of Zen. For that you have to plunge into the practice and taste it for yourself.

David Shoji Scott, Dharma Holder, Kanzeon Sangha

What is Zen?

Zen Buddhism

Buddhism is a simple, practical and highly personal mind-body-spirit discipline. At its core is meditation – uniquely meditation in a sitting position called **za-zen** – which provides a means of engaging on the great question of life and of seeking enlightenment.

"Zen is not mysticism or something esoteric; it is a rational method of helping us become better people."

A.V. Grimstone, *Introduction to Zen Training* by Katsuki Sekida

Zen's first patriarch, **Bodhidharma**, describes Zen in four phrases as being:

1. Outside tradition and outside formal teaching.

2. Without foundation in words or letters.

3. Focused directly on the human mind.

4. Able to see into one's nature and helps you attain Buddhahood.

Zen

The Japanese word Zen comes from the Chinese **ch'an**, which
in turn comes from ancient Indian words **dhyana** and **jhana**.

The word Zen does not have a single, easy definition. In Japan (the
country with which we most associate modern-day Zen practice), it can
mean 'meditation' – which makes sense as it takes elements of
Buddhism and uses them in **za-zen**, with its emphasis on posture and
breathing. The deeper, more mystical translation of Zen is 'revelation'
or 'enlightenment', although there is no precise Western definition for
this essentially Eastern concept.

Buddhism

The word Buddhism is probably more familiar to us than the word Zen.
Buddhism is an Eastern faith, based on the example and teachings of
the Buddha (**c.** 563–483 BC). It has millions of followers worldwide who
belong to a community, the Sangha, a sort of spiritual friendship.
Buddhism has seemingly traditional religious rituals and involves the
study of sacred scripts.

Zen is within the Buddhist tradition, but Zen Buddhism emphasizes the person of the Buddha and what he experienced and said, rather than the communal faith of mainstream Buddhism, with its devotional rituals and sacred-script studies.

What Are We Searching For?

Those practising Zen Buddhism use meditation to clear the mind of material clutter, stripping thoughts away to the point of 'realization' – an all-embracing awareness, 'Buddha nature' or 'Buddhahood', which is the wisdom within us all.

This realization, or awakening, is known as **wu** in Chinese, and **satori** or **kensho** in Japanese. **Satori** and **kensho** are variations on a theme: **satori** is state of enlightenment, a longer-term understanding of what the Buddha understood, **kensho** is more of a sudden grasping, a moment of self-realization – an insight into one's own nature.

"The only Zen you find on the tops of mountains is the Zen you bring up there."
Robert M. Pirsig, *Zen and The Art of Motorcycle Maintenance*

You do not need to be a Zen master or monk to practise Zen Buddhism. In fact all you really need to start is a desire to try, loose-fitting clothes, and a willingness to be a complete novice with the 'beginner's mind' – a clean slate.

Koans

Another aspect of practising meditation, which
is special to Zen Buddhism, is the contemplation
of seemingly simple stories that have intriguingly
dense propositions called **koans**.

Koans are enigmatic stories and question-and-answer
dialogues that Zen Buddhist monks can aspire
to master in a series of stages over 30 years.
They can also be used (as they are
in this book) as a prompt to help
understand the Zen approach to
Buddhism and to enlightenment.

On Another Level

In its free-form, minimalist approach, Zen Buddhism is wholly concerned with the self and with finding reality through realization. This makes Zen Buddhism hard to describe in a rational and reasoned (Western) way. Many of the statements – for example in the **koans** that are given throughout this book – seek to explain what Zen Buddhism seeks, but can seem wilfully non-sensical and exasperating:

'What is the sound of one hand clapping?'

'What was your original face before your parents were born?'

'What colour is the wind?'

In Zen, however, such apparently unsolvable riddles are intentional: it is only by immersing yourself in enigmatic questions that you will be able to open the doors of perception.

Self-Realization & No-Mind

Eihei Dogen (1200-53) was the founder of Japanese Soto Zen.
He wrote:

"To learn about the way of the Buddha is to learn about oneself.
To learn about oneself is to forget oneself.
To forget oneself is to be enlightened by everything in the world.
To be enlightened by everything is to let fall one's own body and mind."

Zen is an experience of 'no-mind' – a fleeting feeling of **mushin** (literally
mu, 'no'; **shin**,'mind', which means 'no ego'). This is a state where the
mind is in balance, as cares, anxieties and pressures are released.

The mind picks up many thoughts, desires, opinions and ideas and is
constantly absorbing and changing. 'No-mind', in contrast, is always
the same – 'from birth to death, this is how it is' (Ma-tsu, Zen master).

The following two Zen stories may help you understand this.

The Fluttering Flag

Two monks were arguing about the temple flag fluttering in the wind.
One said, 'It is the flag that flutters'. The other said, 'It is the wind that
moves'. They argued back and forth but could not agree. Hui-neng the
sixth patriarch (Zen master) said, 'Gentlemen! It is not the flag that
moves. It is not the wind that moves. It is your mind that moves.'
The two monks were awestruck.

The Gateless Gate

There is a story of three monks doing **za-zen** when a famous teacher came in with the tea. One of the monks shut his eyes. The teacher asked, 'Where are you going?'. The monk replied that he was entering the Zen state of awareness or revelation. The teacher responded, '[Zen] has no gate; how can you enter into it?'.

The mind follows an endless path – a 'gateless gate' – through which we journey to understand ourselves and where we are in the perplexing maelstrom of life.

An understanding of the basics of Zen Buddhism can be used in the routine of daily life – as Zen can be practised through meditation, **koan** study, gardening, cooking, flower arranging, even making the tea.

Zen in Action: Awareness – Stop, Be Quiet, Look

Try this simple exercise to get used to the idea of experiencing 'the here and now' – the idea of what Zen Buddhists call the direct experience.

1. For meditation it is better if you wear loose comfortable clothes. This is not a full meditation exercise, however, so you do not need to assume any meditation positions. Just sit on a chair or sofa with your back straight and your feet flat on the floor.

2. Switch off any radios, televisions and other appliances and try to create quiet space.

3. Breathe regularly with slow deep breaths. Hear your breathing. Be as still as you can.

4. For the next few minutes forget about thinking. Try humming at a certain pitch and gaze at what is around you. Do not label things, or think about them, just accept their form, colour and 'presence'.

5. Let what you are gazing at absorb you. Accept each object and acknowledge that you are experiencing all this moment by moment.

6. After five minutes, reflect on your experience. Were you aware of your 'presence' in the here and now?

Zen & Now: History & Development

Understanding Zen's Roots

To get a deeper insight into Zen Buddhism and how it can work for you, it is helpful to know where it came from, how it got to where it is today and where it will take you.

The Buddhism in Zen refers to its roots. Buddhism is one of the great faiths of the world and was around before Islam and Christianity. It follows the life and teachings of the Buddha who lived some 500 years before Jesus and a thousand years before Mohammed.

"When an ordinary man attains knowledge, he is a sage; when a sage attains understanding he is an ordinary man."
David Schiller, **The Little Zen Companion**

Zen Buddhism comes from the ancient eastern cultures of India and China (and later Japan), where not only Buddhism but also the guiding 'way' of Taoism and yoga took hold as well. These systems of beliefs are very un-Western and are primarily concerned with the 'liberation' of the mind, body and spirit.

Buddha

About one in five people follow the teachings of Buddha, who lived in the sixth century BC. Buddha is a title meaning 'the enlightened one', 'the one who knows' and 'the wise'. His real name was Siddhartha Gautama (**c**. 563–483 BC) and he was the son of the rulers of the Kingdom of the Sakyas, a ruling caste in northeast India (present-day Nepal).

Siddhartha had a pampered and sheltered upbringing, and when he did go out into the world he was overwhelmed by the suffering he saw. His life's mission became a longing to overcome the pain of his fellow people and to discover the true meaning of life.

Under the famed Bodhi Tree he meditated for 49 days until he achieved his enlightenment as the Buddha.

Theravada and Mahayana Buddhism

After the Buddha's death, the followers of Buddhism split into two branches. Theravada Buddhism, claiming more ancient traditions, and Mahayana Buddhism, claiming to be the most complete and highest account of the Buddha's teachings. It was this latter branch from which Zen Buddhism evolved.

Karma

Karma is a core belief of Buddhism. It is defined as follows:

"When we act or react from an underlying motive of meanness, defensiveness or acquisitiveness, there are always likely to be unfortunate repercussions. We do not perceive accurately. We create upset or anger in other people. We sabotage our own self-esteem, and store up bad memories in our minds. This is the heart of what Buddhism means by karma. It is useful to be clear about this, because karma is a notion that has been interpreted, especially by Westerners, in a variety of different ways, not all of them accurate. Often karma is taken to mean the results of our unenlightened actions, and in a sense this is true. As ye sow, so shall ye reap. But the results that are referred to are not forfeits doled out by a universe that has a sort of built-in system of retribution, but the everyday costs, in terms of the quality of relationships, and the degree of self-respect we feel, that naturally accrue."

Guy Claxton, *The Heart of Buddhism*

Bodhidharma

After the Buddha, the key mover of Buddhism – for the Zen Buddhist –
is Bodhidharma. He was an Indian monk who carried the Buddha's
teachings from India to China in AD 520 and later became known as the
first Zen patriarch. His 'take' on Buddhism was not about the scriptures,
but all about seeing into one's nature and attaining Buddhahood
through meditation.

Emperor Wu of Liang, who received Bodhidharma in China, was a
devout follower of Buddhism and anxious to seek this new monk's seal
of approval. The story of their meeting does much to explain the
essence of Zen Buddhism (or **ch'an** as it was called in China). Loosely
translated it reads:

Wu began, 'I have built many temples ... and ordained many monks since
becoming Emperor. Therefore I ask you what is my merit?'

'None whatsoever,' answered Bodhidharma.

The Emperor was taken aback: 'Why no merit?'

Bodhidharma explained that such good deeds only brought minor rewards.

'What then is the most important principle of Buddhism?', asked the Emperor.

Bodhidharma replied, 'Vast emptiness, nothing sacred.'

The Emperor was now becoming even more bewildered and unimpressed by this monk, and so asked, 'Who then is this that stands before me?'

Bodhidharma told him: 'I don't know.'

Emperor Wu did not 'get it': he was concerned with short-term good deeds in relation to karma, and a gradual step-by-step approach to a higher level of nirvana (classic Buddhism). Wu was missing out on the teaching of the possibilities of direct and sudden enlightenment and awakening that Bodhidharma had brought with him from India.

Bodhidharma retired to Shaolin monastery where he spent nine years
in meditation staring at a wall. In time, he came to teach monks and
added t'ai chi and Shaolin kung fu to their regime to strengthen their
energies and resolve for meditation. **Ch'an** (from the Sanskrit dhyana,
meaning 'meditation') was now set on a course to become the
meditation version of Buddhism. By the eighth century it was well
established in China thanks to the Zen masters Baso (Ma-tsu, AD 709–88),
his disciple Nan-ch'uan (Nansen AD 748–834), and his successors
Joshu Jushin (Chao-chou or Zhao-zhou, AD 778–897) and Sekito
(Shih-t'ou AD 700–90).

Zen Spreads its Appeal

Zen filtered into mainstream Japanese society, via monks travelling from China, at a time when power lay with the samurai warlords. Zen's stripped-down approach and meditation appealed to this military class who sought spiritual guidance as much as the martial arts of war.

Its practical simplicity and directness also made it attractive to artisans and artists alike, who could apply it to a whole host of disciplines from poetry to archery. The influence of Zen priests from China brought about changes in the style of residential buildings and gardens. The military elite preferred to enjoy their gardens from inside the house, so priest-designers or **ishitateso** (literally, 'rock-placing monks'), came to the fore.

Later, groups of skilled craftsmen called **senzui kawaramono** ('mountain, stream and riverbed people') were responsible for creating a new style of garden, known as **karesansui** ('dry mountain stream'), heavily influenced by Zen Buddhism.

Rinzai and Soto Zen

The founder of Zen in Japan was the monk Eisai (1141–1215), who established the Rinzai (Chinese 'Lin-chi') Zen school in the north in 1198, at monasteries at Kyoto and Kamakura with royal patronage.

It was Eisai who introduced the use of **sanzen**. This was a visit by a monk to a master (called a **roshi**, a term still used today) to discuss a '**koan**' – a seemingly simple story intended to 'switch a light on' in the monk as he meditated on it. **Koans** could not be meditated upon rationally; the monk had to let go and stop straining to 'solve' the words. There was no single correct answer, instead there were many interpretations. **Koans** were given to monks as a series of stages to pass through to encourage the spirit of Zen. The monk concentrated on the **koan** so that he might transcend his mind barriers and achieve **satori** ('enlightenment').

The other main branch of Zen Buddhism in Japan is Soto Zen (Chinese 'tsao-tung'), which was introduced in the south in 1227 by Eihei Dogen. Dogen established a monastery at Eiheiji without imperial favours and promoted the practice of **za-zen** – sitting meditation – to achieve enlightenment through a serene reflective approach. Dogen also laid down many of the rules found in Zen monasteries today. He was author of the **Shobogenzo**, a great work of Zen Buddhist teaching.

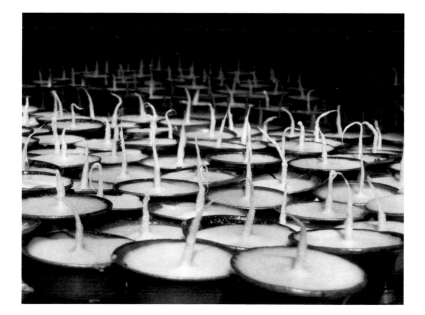

Zen Today

It was D.T. Suzuki (1870–1966) who pioneered Zen Buddhism in the West through his teachings and books. He moved to the USA and taught Zen in New York, where he influenced many Western intellectuals and writers including Carl Jung, J.D. Salinger and Allen Ginsberg.

Zen Buddhism blossomed with the 'Beat Generation' of the 1950s, notably author Jack Kerouac who popularized Buddhist concepts such as karma and **satori**. Zen enthusiast Alan Watts explained **The Way of Zen** (1957) to a whole new generation interested in how it worked, while later still Robert M. Pirsig popularized the term Zen, if not the understanding, with his **Zen and The Art of Motorcycle Maintenance**.

Experience Zen

Today there are many Zen Buddhist meditation centres, halls and abbeys where the essence of Zen can be experienced.

In a modern-day Zen monastery, meditation is still paramount, along with the study of **koans**. **Sesshins**, seven-day retreats, are available for serious students and lay people alike. These take the form of long periods of reflective silence interspersed with a **sanzen**, **za-zen** and walking meditation, meals, rest periods and so on.

Meditation:
The Core of Zen

Zen Meditation

"Meditation is not the
means to an end. It is both
the means and the end."

J. Krishnamurti, spiritual teacher

'Zen' means meditation, and while meditation is important to all forms of Buddhism (as well as to other Eastern ways of seeking inner calm and physical and spiritual wellbeing such as yoga), meditation is absolutely central to Zen Buddhism. In every Zen Buddhist monastery, meditation is practised for several hours every day.

Meditation is a refreshing way to refocus the mind and to sort all the bric-a-brac we store in our head and which gets in the way of thoughts, emotions and sensations. This state of mind is often called 'mindfulness'.

Zen meditation is an experience in itself. To meditate sit with a good posture, concentrate on breathing, and clear your mind of distractions to reach not a state of mind, but no-mind, not a way of thinking but non-thinking.

The Benefits of Meditation

To empty and refocus the mind, and achieve 'no-mind' we also need to be physically receptive and relaxed, so meditation teaches us ways to be still, to breathe, and to deport ourselves and so be in harmony with our surroundings whether sitting, kneeling or standing.

Properly practised meditation brings many benefits in its search for awareness of the 'ultimate reality':

- A sense of empowerment and energy.
- A compassionate and cheerful attitude.
- A feeling of inner peace and wellbeing.
- The ability to focus on anything for longer and longer periods.
- An understanding of the beauty of the world and the value of all things living in it.

Zen is both a practical and spiritual path to understanding through meditation. Meditation also teaches the mind, body and spirit to be still and to gain inner strength and a sense of wellbeing.

Where to Practise

If you are travelling to a place of meditation, whether it is a Buddhist abbey or a village hall, give yourself plenty of time to get there, because you need to arrive in a calm frame of mind.

Assuming that you will not be able to meditate in a cave, as the early Zen Buddhist monks did, or by a beautiful panorama, then be practical and make a space in your home. Zen Buddhism is all about gaining control within the life you lead day to day – gaining control of your mind, or mindfulness, as it is called.

If you are going to meditate in the place where you live, then you have the scope to create a sympathetic ambience. If you are meditating where you work this might not be as easy, but still possible. Do not underestimate the importance of a defined space that you can regularly feel at peace in. Think of the space as a sanctuary: somewhere that you feel calm and do not associate with quarrels or negative situations.

Some define their space as a 'bubble', but what is around you in terms of content is equally important.

Ideal Conditions for Meditation

- Peaceful and quiet places to encourage contemplation.
- Places with average light – not too dark, not overly bright.
- Comfortable temperature.
- Smoke-free, silent environments.

If you want to de-clutter your mind, you certainly want to keep physical clutter to a minimum. If the room is naturally full of objects, perhaps put a simple rug or throw over the shelving or bookcases. Try to keep it as minimalist as possible.

Keep the room comfortably warm not cold. You can use a plant, candles or crystals in appropriate places to gaze at. Simple pictures are fine but nothing too provoking. This is about creating neutral space where the walls will merge into nothingness. You can use certain icons to help prepare you, such as Japanese calligraphy or brush drawing, for instance.

While it is better not to have plumes of smoke or gusts of wind intruding into your meditation space, the use of scented candles and incense sticks can help you re-create each session – a repetitive ritual can trigger a contemplative mind. The smell of pine and cedar is often associated with Zen Buddhist meditation. Some people find the addition of wind chimes or the use of a small bell helps to create the right conditions to prepare for meditation.

When to Practise

Early Morning

The time to practise meditation is down to personal preference and practicalities. Try to make your sessions consistent, however, as a routine will help you to be in a suitable frame of mind. Traditionally sunrise, or just after you have woken up, are considered optimum times for meditation, before the noises of the material world have taken over. Your mind is also fresh from sleep and you have not begun to concentrate about the day and its schedule. Most of all meditation sets you up perfectly for the whole day.

Evening

If morning time is not practical, because you have to rush off to work or get the kids sorted for school, then perhaps the other end of the day is best for you. Evening is perfect for getting ready for bed and, again, the noises of the day have started to subside. At this time you can shed all the worries and concerns that have built up in the day.

After Work

Many people book a regular slot after work, perhaps via the commute home. You need to allow time to include travelling to your class, getting changed, and preparing yourself for meditation.

Lunch and Coffee Breaks

These are another option with a fixed time, but they are generally not as satisfactory for removing distractions and interruptions.

How Long?

A meditation session can last from 5 to 30 minutes – some monastery monks even spend all day in meditation. What is right for you?

5 Minutes

This is the ideal length of time for a beginner's session. It can seem endless when you are normally so used to fidgeting, wanting to do other things and letting your mind worry about something. Most of this time may be taken up with posture and breathing adjustments. However, after some sessions you can find a five minute time slot very refreshing.

10 to 15 Minutes

Up to quarter of an hour gives you time to slow down and adjust to a different internal clock. This provides time for concentration and deepening awareness, as well as time to consider the **koans**.

15 to 30 Minutes

Again there is plenty of time for preparation and closure of the session, as well as a large span for different meditative poses and exercises, as well as consideration of the **koans**, other contemplations and mind-relaxing techniques.

What to Wear

Loose-fitting clothes allow you to breathe, assume positions and stretch easily. While you want clothes to be loose, they should not be skimpy or poorly fitting as they too can act as distractions, especially in a group. Having said that, it is perfectly reasonable in the privacy of your own home to practise meditation naked. As you are alone you might feel nudity best reflects the 'stripped down' aesthetic of Zen without the attachment of clothes, which have associations and could induce mind-wandering thoughts (about shopping for instance). Also, when naked, you will be more in tune with the temperature around you.

If you prefer clothes, try a tracksuit, T-shirt and shorts or a simple kimono-style dressing gown. Preferably your meditation clothes should be freshly washed, as odours can be off-putting. Some Zen groups prefer dark or even black clothing so that it does not distract others meditating, which garish, bright or patterned clothing might do. Above all, you should avoid anything tight fitting.

What to Sit On

Upright Chair

If you are going to use a chair, pick one that has an upright, wooden back and a wooden seat. A dining or kitchen chair is ideal. You can add a cushion for comfort if you like. A little bit of in-built padding or upholstery in the seat is fine, but avoid sofa-style armchairs.

It's easier said than done to sit still. You might be a natural fidgeter, shuffling about, swinging your legs or tapping your heels on the carpet. Maybe you get cramp easily. In any of these situations sitting still for 5 or 10 or 15 minute sessions (or longer) is not easy. After 30 minutes you will want to do stretching and walking exercises for 10 minutes.

Correct posture in an upright, solid seat is important as it will help you overcome physical discomforts and let you concentrate on your upper body.

To choose a seat with the correct height, make sure that when you are sitting the soles of your feet rest flat on the floor (without shoes and preferably without socks as well). Some people put a cushion on the floor for their feet to achieve a suitable posture.

As long as your buttocks are higher than your knees and you are not tilting forward enough to topple over, you are fine. Tilting forward naturally helps you to keep your back straight.

Cushions, Stools and Pillows

There are small, plump, round cushions called **zafus** (meaning 'sitting cushion' in Japanese). These are purpose-made for meditation. The filling should be material that keeps its shape after repeated sittings – kapok (a natural silky fibre) works well. Sometimes **zafus** are put on top of another larger, flattish, square cushion filled with cotton to give extra height. Alternatively a much larger black mat known as a zabuton may be used.

Whichever posture you assume on a cushion, make sure it gives sufficient height so that both knees can touch the floor and your pelvis tilts slightly forward when sitting.

A low meditation stool is another option to sit on while meditating. They are available from yoga centres. There are also fold-away meditation chairs that open up to support the back and allow cross-legged poses.

Modern office 'kneeling' chairs may be handy if you suffer from sore or stiff joints, as they naturally incline you into a kneeling pose without having to kneel on the floor or a cushion.

For people who are frail, infirm or recuperating in bed, you can buy a v-shaped pillow that helps you maintain the correct posture in the upper half of your body.

Zen in Action: Candle Gazing

Some people meditate with eyes shut and many with a half-opened, half-shut gaze. Some need the reassurance of blackness to empty their minds; others can 'let go' while gazing at the material world. There is a tradition among some Zen monks of facing the wall while meditating. Many followers today have a tableau of shop-bought stimuli or the

panorama of a natural vista. Whatever works for you, make sure it does not distract you, but instead enhances your peace of mind.

Visualization is a useful tool to help you meditate, and one of the easiest images to visualize is a flame, whether flickering or still. The more you practise this, the longer you should be able to hold the image. Eventually you will not need the real candle at all.

1. Place a candle in front of you a few feet away at eye level (you are in meditative pose). Make sure it is secure in a holder and on a firm and flat surface.

2. Stare directly at it for a few seconds (you can blink).

3. Close your eyes and keep the image in your mind's eye. Try to hold the flame's shape and glowing nature.

4. If the image fades, open your eyes and look at the flame again to re-establish the link.

5. If your mind starts to wander and fill with thoughts, visualize the thoughts falling into the flame and being consumed.

Zen in Action: Create Your Zen Ritual

Rituals are a prop to help you settle into the right frame of mind, no more and no less. They are not essential, especially in Zen Buddhist meditation, which stresses the practical experiencing of the here and now - stop, be quiet, look.

Nevertheless, for those starting out or struggling to make it work, the use of a few rituals that encourage inner discipline are not to be dismissed. Only you will know how effective they are, so you must monitor them carefully. Try this simple set up:

1. Ring a bell or use a stick against a wind chime to announce the beginning of a session. Do the same at the end of the session.

2. Listen to the sound disappearing slowly and use this as a prompt to empty your mind.

3. Bow in front of your cushion, chair or stool as a mark of respect – after all, it is giving you much-needed support.

4. Before you end the session, use a mantra (short prayer) or saying, such as 'love, devotion and surrender' or 'I take refuge in the Buddha, the Dharma (the Buddhist 'laws' and teachings) and the Sangha (the Buddhist community)'.

Posture Principles

There are a number of postures you can adopt for sitting meditation. They go in order of learning (a bit like beginner, intermediate and expert), but are also chosen according to body suppleness, level of fitness, age, convenience and personal choice.

Sitting on a Chair or Stool

- Sit upright, not slouched.
- Your thighs should be parallel to the floor.
- Hands should be palm-down, open or slightly closed and resting on top of your thighs.
- Feet should face forward and be firmly flat on the floor. If you are tall place a cushion on the seat; if you are short a block of wood or large book could raise up the floor height adequately.
- Hold your head up, but not stiffly, as though a cotton thread is running from it, straight up to the ceiling.
- Focus on an object such as a candle flame or blank wall.

Hand Positions

Rest your hands on your lap or in front of your navel. Have your right hand under the left and facing (or turned) upwards, fingers-first. The thumbs can be slightly touching at the tips. Another stable hand position for meditating comes from grasping the thumb of one hand in the palm of the other, again both palms facing upwards.

Kneeling

You can do **za-zen** meditation kneeling if this is more comfortable for you. This is also a good posture for beginners wanting to learn how to position the lower abdomen correctly. When you push your waist forward in this position, the stress will naturally be thrown into a triangular base of bottom and knees.

Kneel on the floor on a cushion or folded blanket about three feet square. A second smaller and firmer cushion is placed on top of that blanket. Kneel down either side of the cushion so the weight, initially at least, is taken on your knees and shins. Let your buttocks rest directly on top of the cushion to encourage the correct posture and spine position.

Tuck your legs below your thighs and have your feet touching. Your two knees and your bottom effectively make up a triangle, as they should for all the cushion-sitting poses. The upper-body posture (the head, shoulder and hands) is the same as when meditating while sitting in a chair.

Burmese Posture

This is a cross-legged position (arms can be high or low), which is relatively easy and stable to adopt and is therefore the most popular for those starting out on the Zen path to meditation. As with all these postures, you need a cushion or folded blanket about three feet square. A second smaller and firmer cushion is placed on top of that blanket. Sit on the cushion, tilting slightly forward. Bend your left leg and grasp your ankle. Draw your foot in to where your legs meet below the bottom. Now bend your right leg and bring that foot into the 'crevice' you have formed between the calf and thigh of the left leg. Allow both knees to drop and touch the blanket. The cushion should be directly under the bottom only – it should not support the thighs. Again there should be the triangular base of knees and bottom. If both knees are not on the floor, use a firmer, higher cushion, try reversing the leg positions or go back to kneeling or sitting.

Curve your spine forward slightly, letting your tummy hang naturally while your bottom is pushed back for solid support. Slump at all, and you lose the position and the grounding.

The pelvis should be tilted forward a little and held firmly fixed in this position. Then hold your head up, chin in, and eyes slightly open and cast down. Place your hands in your lap in the first hand position from page 74. The upper body should be as in previous poses.

When we say straight back, this does not mean the spine, which is not held in a straight line. If you looked at a **za-zen** position in cross section, the spine would be more like an elongated 'S' or gently curving snake shape.

Take care not to fall into what is called the tailor position (because tailors traditionally use it), in which the waist is lowered backward, the knees do not touch the floor and the pose does not support a straight back. If you tilt backwards, your lower back will become tired. Your waist should always be pushed forward to allow for relaxation in the upper body.

Half Lotus

This is an uneven sitting position which tends to pull the spine out of line, raising one shoulder above the other. However, it is a lot easier than the full lotus and offers a stable pose in which the right foot goes under the left thigh resting on the cushion, and the left foot is on the right thigh. The reverse of this is also possible and it makes sense to alternate the legs. Make sure both knees are on the cushion. Using a mirror in front of you can help correct the tilting.

Full Lotus

Imagine a mighty pine grounded in the mountain terrain, expressing a sense of dignity and grandeur. So too with the full lotus position, which gives the greatest stability and 'grounding' and is really one for the initiated meditator. Flexibility and stretching exercises are needed for this (and probably a meditation teacher) and the novice will find it uncomfortable to maintain, and therefore distracting.

Kinhin: Walking Meditation

You can also meditate while walking. Zen Buddhist monks practise walking in a mindful state, in between sitting meditation sessions. It is called **kinhin**, and the rhythmic physical activity of walking can enhance the experience of being in the 'here and now'.

Zen in Action: Walk with Zen Meditation

1. Place your right fist, thumb inside, in front of your chest. Cover over the fist with your left palm. Your elbows should be at right angles to, and slightly away from, your body.

2. Straighten your body so the chin is drawn in and your neck is straight. Allow your gaze to wander a few metres in front of you.

3. Step a half step forward instead of taking a full stride. This step is designed to last one breath so you can co-ordinate your breathing with your walking.

4. Raise the rear foot as you inhale and bring it past your stationary foot and down sole-first as you exhale. Think of sinking your foot as though on gravel (rather than a hard surface), so as to feel the sensation of the ground beneath your feet much more vividly.

5. Walk quietly in a straight line, avoiding right or left turns until you are ready to come back.

Zen in Action: Standing Meditation

1. Stand legs apart, at ease facing forward.

2. Drop your arms to each side with palms facing backwards.

3. Close your eyes and empty your mind of preoccupations.

4. Remain in this posture for several minutes, then rub your hands together as though to warm them.

5. As you open your eyes, dab the palms of your hands on them, rub your face and walk about briskly.

Breathing

The act and awareness of breathing has always been a focus
for meditation. In **za-zen**, the rise and fall of the abdomen, our muscle
tone, our attention, wakefulness and breathing are all considered. We
are 'mindful' of our inhalations and exhalations, even though breathing
can be an automatic, unconscious activity. In Zen meditation, breathing
in **za-zen** is a complete practice that requires full concentration.

Counting Breaths

You can begin **za-zen** by counting breaths. This is not as easy
as it sounds, so do not be disappointed if it takes time (minutes,
weeks, months, years) to get a rhythm going and block out all the
thoughts trying to crowd in. You are trying to occupy your mind with
your breathing so that random thoughts cannot get in. You will have to
keep restarting from 'one' plenty of times!

1. When you inhale, count 'one' inwardly.

2. When you exhale, count 'two' outwardly and so on up to 10.

3. Return to one and repeat the sequence, perhaps just whispering or concentrating on the numbering internally.

4. Vary this and now count, on the in breath only, one to 10. Breathe out without counting these breaths.

5. Now count on the out breath only. Let the intake of breath pass without counting.

Koans

A monk was bowing before a statue of the Buddha. Joshu Jushin (Chao-chou or Zhao-zhou), a Zen master of the T'ang Dynasty in China, slapped him.

The monk, taken aback, exclaimed, 'Is it not praiseworthy to bow before the Buddha?'

'Yes but it is better to do without even a praiseworthy thing,' replied Joshu.

Koans like this are remarkable stories, anecdotes, problems devised by ancient Zen masters to stop their students' minds wandering and to prevent them endlessly trying to define and grasp everything with words.

Koans are both superficially exasperating and deeply meaningful. You might see the point immediately or not at all. Its effect is like a joke without the punch line – you stand there puzzled, thinking 'I do not get it'. You cannot find the 'answer' you seek – you then give up and the answer comes by itself. **Koans** should not be taken literally. **Koans** are not words, they are states of mind and a Zen way to meditation.

Classic Koans

Many of the **koans** were compiled in classic collections, the two most famous being **Mu-mon-kan**, meaning 'no-gate-barrier' or 'the gateless gate', and **Hegikanroku**, 'the blue cliff record'. **Mu-mon-kan** – from which excerpts follow – was compiled by the Chinese Zen master Ekai (also called Mumon, 1183–1260).

Joshu Washes the Bowl

A Zen monk asked his Zen master Joshu, 'I have just entered the monastery, please teach me.'

The Zen master responded 'Have you eaten your gruel?' The monk replied that he had.

'Then you had better wash your bowl,' continued the master, and the monk was enlightened.

The Path

Joshu asked his teacher Nansen, 'What is the path?'

'Everyday life is the way,' Nansen replied. 'Can it be studied?' asked Joshu.

'If you try to study, you will be far away from it,' responded Nansen.

'If I do not study how can I know it is the path?' persisted Joshu.

Nansen continued that the true path was not a matter of knowing or not knowing. Knowing was delusion; not knowing was senseless. If he wanted to reach the true way beyond doubt, this would be impossible as it was like the great void, so dark and boundless.

'How could there be a right or wrong in the way?' After this Joshu came to a sudden realization.

Joshu's Dog

One of the shortest and most repeated **koans** goes like this:

A monk asked Zen master Joshu: 'Does a dog have Buddha nature or not?' The Zen master answered, '**Mu**'. (**Mu** is the negative symbol in Chinese meaning 'No-thing', or 'nay'.)

What does this mean? Firstly it is about throwing out all your preconceptions that you need to find an answer. The question is both so trivial yet so mind-expanding that a simple 'yes' or 'no' should not be given. The Buddha nature cannot be captured by yes or no. 'Unask the question' is how you might interpret it.

One Zen master believed that to realize Zen, 'You must work through every bone in your body, through every pore in your skin, filled with this question: What is **Mu**? And carry it night and day.'

Zen in Action: Working on a Koan

The exercise of working on a **koan** is no fast track to becoming a Zen master. It is trying to help you see that the **koan** does not have a right or wrong answer; it is the answer.

Consider the **koan** about the Buddha-nature of a dog while you are in a meditative posture. You will have thoughts like: if all living things have Buddha-nature, why did the Zen master say '**Mu**' (no) about the dog?

Repeat the word '**Mu**' to yourself in the process of breathing out. Feel the abdomen caving by degrees. Then inflate from the bottom of the abdomen and begin to breathe in.

Go beyond the thought of what '**Mu**' means – neither no nor yes.

Concentrate your energy into this '**Mu**' and go into your Buddha-nature. '**Mu**' is an affirmation of Buddha-nature not a negative put-down. It is above and beyond rational thought and conventional perception.

Zen Mondo

A classic Zen method of instruction between master and monk was the **mondo** (Chinese **wen-ta**) or 'question-and-answer' dialogue. Here are some much-quoted Zen dialogues to consider.

We Dress; We Eat

A famous Zen master was asked, 'We dress and eat everyday, how do we escape from having to put on clothes and eat food?'

The master answered the monk, 'We dress; we eat'.

'I do not understand,' said the monk.

'If you do not understand, put on your clothes and eat your food.'

The Jug of Water

Hyakujo wished to send a monk to open a new monastery. He told his pupils that whoever answered a question most ably would be appointed. Placing a jug of water on the ground, he asked, 'Who can say what this is without calling its name?'

The head monk said, 'No one can call it a wooden sandal.' Isan, the cooking monk, tipped over the jug with his foot and went out. Hyakujo grinned and said, 'The head monk loses.' And Isan became master of the new monastery.

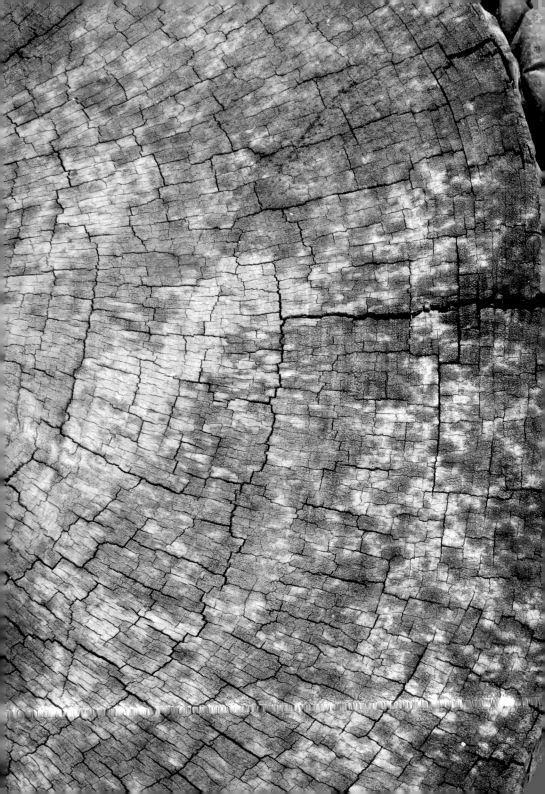

LivingZen

Space and Simplicity: the Zen Way

A key appeal of Zen to people in the furiously paced, consumer-driven West is its simplicity – its seeking of a stripped-down, clutter-free approach to life, where less is more, space is central and time is as much as you set aside.

The beauty of Zen is not just in its pared-down meditative and spiritual approach to life, but also in the application of its minimalist approach to the many practical, everyday things you do.

You can tap into Zen Buddhism as a way to relax, to perform gentle martial arts and even to steer you in pursuit of sporting excellence. You can apply it to guide you in laying out your home interior spaces and designing your garden. You can even practise Zen in your approach to cooking, flower arranging and serving tea.

Zen and the Home

Traditional Japanese houses were influenced by the guiding hand of Zen in contemplation and calmness, combined with the natural Japanese love of sparsity. They have open spaces, clean lines and geometric shapes, as well as a sense of harmony between the private interior and the garden exterior, a wooden veranda sometimes linking the two.

While it may be idealistic to expect a sudden transformation from muddled, lived-in, child-friendly Western interiors to austere, architect-orientated settings, you could aim to achieve a 'Zen' space where you can meditate, allowing one room to be clutter-free. Ask yourself, 'What can I leave out?', rather than 'How can I fill that space?'.

Storage

Space, light, order and openness are key to Zen spirit in the home. A simple way to achieve this is to buy or build simple storage spaces. Basic cupboards with sliding doors are the traditional Japanese way of keeping things uncluttered. Installing a rail for clothing and boxes for books, CDs and DVDs in an alcove or recess and fixing a blind or curtain in front will do just as well. In this way you continue the sense of space, continuity and fluidity around the room.

Another storage option is a simple square or oblong trunk or chest (in Japan these are traditionally made of natural wood such as pine) in which you can store possessions.

Screens

In Japan, traditional sliding latticework panels covered with translucent white rice paper are used to screen off areas and create inner-room partitions. **Shoji** screens as they are called – or variations on that design – can be purchased at most furniture shops. Use such a screen to cover an unsightly interior, storage or shelving areas or to divide a living, working or sleeping area. That way you can create a secluded Zen meditation space, either on an ad hoc or a more permanent basis.

Flooring

In traditional Japanese homes, plain **tatami** straw mats are used on the floor. Often beige in colour, they are traditionally made of tightly packed straw, with two cloth borders and a rush cover. They offer a surprising amount of insulation and comfort.

Practising monks sleep and practise **za-zen** meditation on such a mat in a living space linking the dormitory and the meditation hall. The size of the mat is similar to a single mattress size, so two **tatami** together could form the basis of a double futon or meditation area closed by a **shoji** screen.

Guiding Forms

There are three Zen-inspired concepts that inform Japanese cultural life, especially design and architecture, and can guide your interior planning:

- **Shibui**: highlights simplicity and quality of materials.

- **Wabi**: stresses the subdued natural beauty that is in the very simplicity of an object.

- **Sabi**: focuses on a sense of refined and well-used elegance as seen in a Zen tea-ceremony teapot, or the hilt of a Zen sword.

戒定慧

Zen and Gardening

"Sitting quietly doing nothing Spring comes and the grass grows by itself."

Zen saying

How many gardeners could not agree with this saying from the great Japanese poet Bashō (1644-94)?

LivingZen

The Zen Style

Groups of skilled craftsmen called **senzui kawaramono** ('mountain, stream and riverbed people') were responsible for creating a new style of garden, known as **karesansui** ('dry mountain stream'). Heavily influenced by Zen Buddhism, groups of rocks represent mountains or waterfalls, and white sand is used to replace flowing water. This form of garden, not seen in any other part of the world, was probably influenced by Chinese ink-painted landscapes of barren mountains and dry riverbeds. Examples include the rock garden at the temples of Ryoanji and Daitokuji, both in Kyoto.

Zen gardens are not to everyone's taste – the apparent random positioning of unhewn rocky outcrops, some covered in moss, and the linear shaping of gravel are austere to those used to a profusion of borders and colour and wide expanses of lawn. They might appeal more perhaps to those in Mediterranean and Californian climates, where rock and gravel gardens and succulent plants are the norm.

Western gardening is so much about statement and flourishes and cramming empty spaces with some eye-catching arrangement.

Zen gardens are the opposite. They are about reducing the number of elements to a minimum and using the spaces between to create a harmonious experience. They are about soothing the senses rather than stimulating them.

The Yin-Yang Garden

Balance and harmony are the heart of the Zen garden, reflecting the Tao symbol of yin and yang: the two opposing forces of nature – male/female, outer/inner, darkness/lightness. The opposites are harmonious, however, because they are mutually interdependent. They balance and maintain harmony. The dark and light coloured halves are mirror images making up a whole. In each half there is a tiny circle containing the other half's colour. This symbolizes that one cannot exist without the other, that yin and yang are inseparable.

So it is in the garden – yin is represented by sand and gravel. Zen gardens are dry, so this takes the place of water, which is a 'soft' yin element. This is counterbalanced by the 'hard' yang elements of rock or clumps of bamboo.

Individual rock groupings are planted to create harmonious shapes such as triangles, though it may be very subtle. The rocks are also symbolic of the mountains where the monks went to meditate, so these rocks are not just positioned on top but rooted firmly below the ground level of the garden.

Types of Zen Garden

There are several types of Zen garden today:

- **Tsukiyama** or landscape with a pond or hill. This garden is designed around a meandering path that has stepping stones and bridges that pass over a stream or pond. The views change at each bend.

- **Karesansui** or dry rock with gravel or sand (the archetypal Zen garden). Specifically designed, almost 'brush-painted' for contemplation, these gardens are inward-looking, simplistic, three-dimensional representations of grand Japanese landscapes of misty mountains, gorges, waterfalls and forests. Ryoanji, created with just 15 rocks and white sand on a flat piece of ground, is also typical of flat-style gardens, whose motif was taken from the sea, lakes and ponds.

- **Chaniwa** or tea garden. Tea gardens were developed in conjunction with the tea ceremony, as taught by Sen no Rikyu. It was through the tea garden, which avoided artificiality and was created so as to retain a highly natural appearance, that one

approached the tea house. Elements included stepping stones, stone lanterns, and clusters of trees. The simply designed gazebos in which guests are served tea also have their origin in the tea garden. They were planted at the end of the roji, or dewy path. The tea house was modelled on a monk's rustic retreat. Often there would be a tsukubai, a constantly replenished water basin surrounded by carefully placed stones. The fresh water is used to make the tea. All this condensed the experience of a monk walking through the mountains to a hideaway.

Elements of the Zen Garden

Bamboo

Bamboo is an extraordinarily versatile plant. It can be used to make a shelter with pillars and roof, adapted for a rake, a fishing pole, a storage container or a flower vase. In a Japanese tea ceremony it is used for stirring and scooping. Above all, bamboo has a natural rustic beauty very much in keeping with Zen. The sound of bamboo leaves rustling in the wind or raindrops striking the shoots is highly evocative.

Lotus

The lotus is an iconic plant in Zen, because it is a symbol of peace and perfection. It is also the name of the **za-zen** sitting position – an open, receptive, beautifully balanced and rooted stance.

Raking

The raked sand or gravel in a Zen garden is an important and distinctive feature. Traditionally the carefully raked patterns of sand in a classic Zen garden represent the ebb and flow of nature – for instance patterns raked around rock outcrops symbolize the way of water flowing around an obstacle. The sand or gravel represents the underlay not just of the Zen space, but of the Zen being, of mindfulness. Raking the contours shows how the mind wanders and is distracted by intrusive thoughts. The repetitive action of raking can help empty the mind of thoughts and create the Zen mood of non-thinking.

Zen and Flower Arranging

The art of flower arranging, for it is an art, is called **ikebana** in Japan. It is closely entwined with Zen because it is a manifestation (like raking the gravel, or making the tea) of the pursuit and development of mental composure and, through that, the contemplation of our inner nature. It is a natural way to help focus the mind because it is so superficially simple and refined, yet so deeply complicated, working on many levels. By concentrating on this quiet and natural interplay you are unconsciously emptying your mind and filling it with no-mind. Flower arranging is also part of creating a Zen living space and can be an integral part of your meditation area.

The choice of flowers is down to personal taste, seasonal availability and cost, but more exotic varieties such as orchids or birds of paradise, cut sunflowers, morning glory and snake grass work well. Red roses and pink peonies are also effective.

The key to Zen expression and experience is in the relationship between your patient contemplation and the forms you arrange. Allow time and space to express this even though it is a largely spontaneous act. Do not cram the plants or allow them to be obscured.

Zen and Cooking

The Zen tradition touches all parts of day-to-day living and this applies to the kitchen as much as to the garden or tea house. The ancient Zen monks took as much care and attention in their food preparation as in their **za-zen** preparation. Dogen wrote two reference works much studied in the monasteries: **A Guide for the Kitchen Supervisor** and **Instructions for the Zen Cook**.

It was an old monastery cook who showed the gifted Zen master and monk Dogen a fundamental Zen way. Dogen had just arrived from China at a Japanese port. The cook turned up at the ship to buy Japanese mushrooms. Dogen asked him to stay awhile and talk but the cook insisted he had to get back to his kitchen to cook. Dogen was a bit taken aback and asked the cook why he did not practise **za-zen** and leave the cooking to younger monks. The cook berated Dogen; did not the newly arrived, naive Japanese monk know anything about the spirit of Zen?

Dogen came to realize that Zen Buddhism was all about the everyday and the ordinary:

'Each and every extraordinary activity is simply having rice.'

Zen Monastery Food

The Zen style of cooking is called **shojin ryori**, which loosely means 'spiritual wellbeing through vegetarian cooking', though followers of Zen Buddhism do not have to be vegetarians. Meat-eating is not forbidden by the Buddhist precepts, but as life is about compassion for

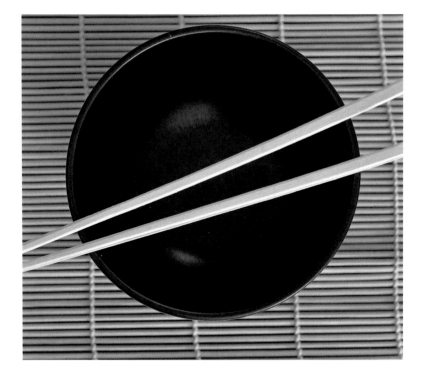

one's fellow beings, it is not encouraged. So you must make sure you make up the shortfall in protein, carbohydrates, vitamins and minerals from missing out on meat.

The monk in charge of the monastery kitchen is the **tenzo** – a highly responsible and important role. They prepare and cook food according to Zen guidelines, as follows:

- To harmonize the six tastes: bitter, sour (or vinegary), sweet, hot, salty and delicate (or soft, as in tofu).
- To develop flavours in the mouth rather than 'hit' the eater on the first mouthful.
- To balance taste, texture, nutrition and diet.
- To prepare with total absorption – so the rice is washed and inspected to be totally free of grit and chaff, the vegetables washed and the pots boiled.
- To waste nothing.
- To do everything with total love.

Three-bowl cooking

Three-bowl cooking is a traditional way of serving food in a Zen monastery, and has practical applications in the modern Western kitchen. There should be:

- One bowl for carbohydrates such as pasta, rice, potatoes.
- One small bowl for protein such as tofu, pulses or dairy food.
- One small bowl for a salad, fruit salad or vegetables.

The monks eat according to **oriyoki**, which means 'containing just enough' – another fine principle for the Western diet to follow.

Zen for Inner Strength: T'ai chi

T'ai chi ch'uan is one of the most popular exercise systems coming from the Chinese and Japanese traditions of martial arts. It originated in China over 2,000 years ago and developed into a set pattern of postures and movements that connect and flow into each other to produce 'moving meditation'. In its slow, deliberate movements and 'total mindfulness' it is a natural preparation for Zen, even when applied to self-defence skills.

T'ai chi means 'great polarity boxing', and the ideal yin and yang – the apparently opposing, but complementary forces – are fundamental to the release of energy flow. Basically it is an exercise system that channels physical energy to improve balance, stability and flexibility towards spiritual strength and contemplation. It also happens to be a great way to reduce tension. The beauty of **t'ai chi** is that you do not have to be athletic to practise it. In fact you need to be relaxed and feel yourself 'sinking' into each posture with a sense of precision to what is called the **tan t'ien** point, two-fingers' width below the navel where energy is said to be stored in the abdomen.

There is total concentration on the movements in the muscles, joints, ligaments and bones and the body revolves around 'sinking' movements combined with slow, deep breathing from the diaphragm.

Zen in Action: Horse-riding Stance

This basic position arises from the ancient martial arts tradition of Shaolin kung fu, originally a fighting and self-defence discipline adopted by Bodhidharma to strengthen the monks at Shaolin monastery. Today it includes many of the techniques of other martial arts, including the punches of karate, the kicks of tae kwon do, and the throws of judo.

You need a trained teacher to take any martial arts seriously, but you can try this quite tiring stance to understand the idea of **ki** (Japanese) or **qi** (Chinese), 'breath' or 'life force'.

1. Stand with your feet apart at shoulder width, keeping your body upright and relaxed.

2. Clench your fists, drawing them in at either side of your waist.

3. Bend your knees, keeping your back straight, and lower your body as though riding on horseback. Empty your mind, 'placing' your thoughts in your lower abdomen.

4. Hold this position for a minute, if you can, breathing deeply. Release the stance if you feel strained.

Zen in Action: Standing Zen

Another stretching exercise to encourage overall energy flow before meditating and to help with breath control and visualization techniques is this 'lifting the sky' exercise.

1. Stand with feet fairly close together, arms straight by your side.

2. Place both your hands palm down, fingers just touching end to end in front of you at navel level.

3. With arms still straight, raise your palms in a continuous arc forward and upward until your palms face the sky. Hold this pose and count to three. Try to inhale slowly through the nose.

4. Slowly lower your arms in a large continuous arc, exhaling slowly, until your arms rest at your side. Repeat the whole sequence six times.

Zen and the Art of Tea

Legend has it that once during meditation Bodhidharma fell asleep and was so angry with himself that he cut off his eyelids and they fell to the ground, where the first tea plant arose. From then until now tea has been sipped by the monks as a protection against falling asleep. It keeps the head clear and invigorates the mind, hence the saying, 'the taste of Zen [**ch'an**] and the taste of tea [**ch'a**] are the same'. Certainly the closeness of the two words in Chinese is interesting.

The Tea Ceremony

Serving tea is as pared down as Zen itself. Traditionally the ceremony takes place in a simple, spartan thatched hut known as the 'abode of vacancy'. The room is framed by a **tatami** and **shoji** and a fire-pit. There is an alcove called a **tokonoma** in which a scroll of calligraphy or spray of flowers is arranged. Utensils are basic.

The ceremony begins with the special kettle literally singing, creating a tranquil phonic welcome (replicating the sound of water rushing or wind blowing). The ceremony has meticulous methods, including how the finely powdered green tea is whisked with bamboo and poured and served and how the drink should be given and received.

Zen in Action: Contemplating Tea

The tea ceremony is not really about pouring tea; it is about the idea of pouring one's conscious thinking and being into this one activity so that it expands infinitely in the present. It imbues – and acts as a foretaste to – many other disciplines associated with Zen such as gardening, pottery and the art of flower arranging.

1. Place a cup (not a mug) of hot tea in front of you while you are in a **za-zen** position.

2. Study the outside of the cup – its shape, its colour, its contours, how it sits or stands on the table: how defined, how stable is it? It appears constant with form.

3. Now gaze at the inside and see it both as an interior and as a mass of fluid form. Is there vapour rising from the surface?

4. Consider the relationship between the hard and the soft, the seen and the unseen, filling and then receiving, the emptiness and the fullness.

This can help you to empty your mind and focus on a single experience.

"To attain the ultimate in art you must master the

mystery of things and then forget that mystery"

Ike No Taiga

Zen Art

Zen is very much in the real world, and you can see it expressed all about you in paintings, poetry, food and flower displays, garden and interior design and architecture. Looking at Zen art offers a very user-friendly way to help us understand Zen.

Zen art is not symbolic art, as with the Chakras or overly religious depictions of the Buddha or the great Zen masters. It is a simple expression of organic living, nature and the world.

Zen and the Art of Calligraphy

Calligraphy is the bold, vigorous brush strokes of black ink on paper or silk, sometimes with poetry and painting combined. Not all calligraphy is Zen-related, but Zen and calligraphy are close to each other in their spontaneous approach to an empty mind and a blank canvas.

The artist uses the ink brush to be expressive, sometimes using meditation to achieve clear, sharp lines with vivid expression. A beautiful image may result, but that is not the objective. The empty space is as important as the swirling lettering or image of a sword or flower. The artist holds the brush upright – there is no resting of the wrists on the paper or silk – and there can be no second tries. It is immediate and without correction; the first stroke is the final stroke.

A Purity of Line

In its simplest form, Zen Buddhist teaching asks us to live in the moment, to be open to our surroundings, to clear the mind and achieve awareness. This seems to be tailor-made for the artist and especially for the calligrapher. Zen calligraphers clear their desks and minds of distractions before picking up the pen.

Their ability to make a pure line is helped by the philosophy that a line is no more than a series of consecutive points, painted in each moment. Again the emphasis is to stay in the present.

Zen Artists

Yamaoka Tesshu (1836–88) was a master in Zen swordsmanship and calligraphy who believed that calligraphy, swordsmanship and **kendo** are identical in leading to the state of 'no-mind'. He was inspired by the way of Hitsuzendo – the practice of Zen through writing with the brush.

Hakuin Ekaku (1686–1769) was one of the most influential Zen monks of the past 500 years, who trained nearly 100 successors in Zen. Hakuin revitalized Rinzai Zen at Shoinji temple, where he used **koan**, calligraphy and painting to reach out to students. His Zen philosophy to art would be, 'Fix yourself in the best place; know exactly where to stop'.

D.T. Suzuki (1870–1966) was a scholar, a revered Buddhist and the great twentieth-century proponent of, and authority on, Zen Buddhism in the West. He moved to the USA in 1897 to teach and influenced many Western intellectuals and writers including Carl Jung and Allen Ginsberg. Suzuki became proficient in calligraphy, with a spontaneous yet graceful brush stroke.

Ike No Taiga (1723-76) was a talented and versatile painter and calligrapher who studied under Hakuin in Kyoto. His understanding of Zen is reflected in his statement that: 'To attain the ultimate in art you must master the mystery of things and then forget that mystery.' Below is his **Tower with Landscape, c.**1740.

Poetry and Haikus

"When you meet a man who is a master swordsman, show him your sword. When you meet a man who is not a poet, do not show him your poem."
Lin-chi

Zen poetry, like Zen painting and Zen flower arranging, is about capturing the essence of an object. **Haikus** are a form of Japanese poetry closest in spirit to the approach of Zen.

A haiku is brief, perhaps the shortest form of poetry known, yet it opens up a visual world that can be meditated upon deeply and endlessly.

A classic **haiku** is typically a three-line, 17-syllable verse with five syllables in line one, followed by seven in line two, and five syllables in line three. The exact number of syllables can vary as they are lost or gained in translation from the Japanese.

Haikus appear preoccupied with the minutiae of nature and seasons – the crane's wings, the fall of snow, a still pond – but they are bound up with **sabi** (a solitary mood reflecting the beauty in simplicity) and **wabi** (an emptiness suddenly filled with a seemingly ordinary object, yet incredible in its ordinariness). As with the other Zen arts, a **haiku** knows when to stop.

Matsuo Bashō

Bashō (1644–94) was a great Japanese poet who elevated the **haiku** into an art form and added the spirit of Zen. Other notable poets were Buson, Issa, Ryōkan and Shiki.

Read the **haikus** that follow and absorb them. Do not try to figure them out, however puzzling they seem. This is Zen – **haikus** are for the here and now – they are not for instruction or relevance. As soon as they exist, they cease to exist.

Very brief
Gleam of blossoms in the treetops
On a moonlit night

Bashō

In the dark forest
A berry drops
The sound of water

Bashō

On a withered branch
A crow is perched,
In the autumn evening.

Bashō

151

Ah! the old pond

A frog jumps in

Sound of water

Bashō

In this famous **haiku**, the pond might be life, still and serene, hence the 'ah!'. Now think of the mind like an ocean; when the wind comes it whips up spume and waves; when the wind dies down the waves recede until the ocean is becalmed and flat as a mirror and then you can see the world reflected in it.

Now reflect that an ordinary creature, a frog, suddenly jumps in breaking both the stillness of water and the stillness of sound (it might be a 'plop') - it resonates the whole universe in a moment of Zen awakening.

Yosa Buson

Along with Bashō and Kobayashi Issa, Yosa Buson (1716–84) is considered among the greatest poets of the Edo Period.

The butterfly
Resting upon the temple bell
Asleep

Yosa Buson

The sea at springtime.
All day it rises and falls,
yes, rises and falls.

Yosa Buson

As you read this poem aloud, do you feel the rise and fall of the waves?

Zen and the Arts

All these disciplines are inspired by the spirit of
Zen and performed in a meditative way.

Do	the Zen way
ka do	the Zen way of flowers
Sa do	the Zen tea ceremony
ken do	the Zen way of the sword
kyu do	the Zen way of archery
Ju do	the Zen way of self defence
ka do	the Zen way of poetry
Sho do	the Zen way of calligraphy

Resources

The author would like to acknowledge the following sources for inspiration and reference:

Books

Barrett, T.H., **Zen – The Reason of Unreason**, HarperCollins, 1993 (The Little Wisdom Library)

Bodian, Stephan, **Meditation for Dummies**, Wiley Publishing Inc., 1999

Durden, Jo, **The Essence of Buddhism**, Eagle Editions, 2004

Fontana, David, **Learn Zen Meditation**, Duncan Baird Publishers, 2001

Hendy, Jenny, **Zen In Your Garden**, Godsfield Press, 2001

Jarmey, Chris, **Book of Meditation**, Element Books/HarperCollins, 2001

Kit , Wong Kiew, **The Complete Book of Zen**, Element Books, 1998

McFarlane, Stewart, **The Complete Book of T'ai Chi**, Dorling Kindersley, 1997

Nishi, Harumi, **Zen Flowers**, Anness Publishing, 2001

Pirsig, Robert M., **Zen and The Art of Motorcycle Maintenance**, Bodley Head, 1974

Reps, Paul (compiler), **Zen Flesh, Zen Bones**, Pelican Books, 1971 (The Charles E. Thuttle Co Inc 1957)

Schiller, David, **The Little Zen Companion**, Workman Publishing Inc., 1994

Scott, David; and Doubleday, Tony, **The Elements of Zen**, Element Books, 1992

Scott, David, **Easy-to-use Zen**, Vega [Chrysalis] Books, 2002

Sekia, Katsuki, **Zen Training: Methods and Philosophy**, Shambhala Publications Inc., 1985

Suzuki, D.T., **Manual of Zen Buddhism**, Rider Books, 1983

Terayama, Prof. Tanchu, **Zen Brushwork: Focusing the Mind with Calligraphy and Painting**, Kodansha International Ltd, 2003

Watts, Alan W., **The Way of Zen**, Pantheon Books, 1957

Websites

The world wide web has a cornucopia of zen-related sites and, as with other subject areas, it is very hit-and-miss. Rather than recommend specific sites I suggest trying random searches through your favourite search engine. However, the following are of note:

news.bbc.co.uk/1/hi/technology/2283398.stm

www.stonewaterzen.org

www.throssel.org.uk

13 AH.